SUPER
SOLAR SYSTEM

Collector Card

SUPER
SOLAR SYSTEM

Collector Card

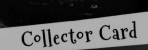

SUPER
SOLAR SYSTEM

Collector Card

SUPER
SOLAR SYSTEM

Collector Card

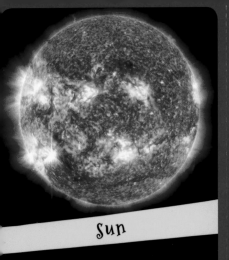

Sun

Our closest star has been shining for 4.6 billion years.

		SCORE
DIAMETER: 865,000 mi. (1.4 m km)		10
MI. (KM) FROM SUN: 0		0
SURFACE TEMP: 9900 °F (5500°C)		10
NUMBER OF MOONS: 0		0

Mercury

This rocky planet near the Sun has very hot days and cold nights.

		SCORE
DIAMETER: 3032 mi. (4880km)		1
MI. (KM) FROM SUN: 36 (58) million		1
SURFACE TEMP 332 °F (167°C)		7
NUMBER OF MOONS: 0		0

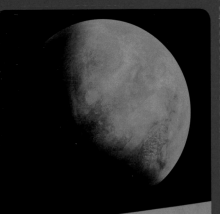

Venus

Some of the many volcanoes on this planet are over 62 mi. (100km) wide.

		SCORE
DIAMETER: 7520 mi. (12,100km)		3
MI. (KM) FROM SUN: 67.2 (108.2) million		2
SURFACE TEMP: 867 °F (464°C)		9
NUMBER OF MOONS: 0		0

Earth

A beautiful warm planet with water to drink and air to breathe.

		SCORE
DIAMETER: 7920 mi. (12,750km)		3
MI. (KM) FROM SUN: 93 (150) million		3
SURFACE TEMP: 59 °F (15°C)		5
NUMBER OF MOONS: 1		1

It's all about . . .

SUPER SOLAR SYSTEM

KINGFISHER

NEW YORK

KINGFISHER
LONDON & NEW YORK

Copyright © Macmillan Publishers International Ltd 2016
Published in the United States by Kingfisher,
175 Fifth Ave., New York, NY 10010
Kingfisher is an imprint of Macmillan Children's Books, London
All rights reserved.

Distributed in the U.S. and Canada by Macmillan,
175 Fifth Ave., New York, NY 10010

Library of Congress Cataloging-in-Publication
data has been applied for.

Series editor: Sarah Snashall
Series design: Little Red Ant
Adapted from an original text by Hannah Wilson

ISBN 978-0-7534-7267-5

Kingfisher books are available for special promotions
and premiums. For details contact: Special Markets
Department, Macmillan, 175 Fifth Ave.,
New York, NY 10010.

For more information, please visit
www.kingfisherbooks.com

Printed in China

9 8 7 6 5 4 3 2 1

1TR/1115/WKT/UG/128MA

Picture credits
The Publisher would like to thank the following for permission to reproduce their material.
Top = t; Bottom = b; Center = c; Left = l; Right = r
Cover Shutterstock/Vadim Sadovski; Back cover NASA; Pages 2–3, 30–31 Shutterstock/Traveller
Martin; 4 Shutterstock/PaulPaladin; 5 Shutterstock/Dudarev Mikhail; 6–7 Kingfisher Artbank;
8–9 Shutterstock/USBFCO; 9 Kingfisher Artbank; 10 Shutterstock/MarcelClemens;
11 Shutterstock/GK; 12–13 Shutterstock/PavleMarjanovic; 12 Shutterstock/Lilkar;
14–15 NASA; 16–17 Shutterstock/Traveller Martin; 17 NASA/JPL; 18–19 NASA/JPL-Caltech/
MSSS; 18 NASA/Hubble Heritage Team (STScl/AURA); 20 Shutterstock/Kirschner;
21–22 Shutterstock/MarcelClemens; 23 Shutterstock/Shalygin; 23b NASA; 24 Shutterstock/
EpicStockMedia; 25t NASA/JPL-Caltech; 25b NASA/ESA/Caltech; 26t NASA/EIT/SOHO/ESA;
26c NASA/Hubble Heritage Team (STScl/AURA); 26b NASA/Walt Feimer; 27 Kingfisher Artbank;
28 Shutterstock/Prometheus72; 29 NASA/STScl; 29b NASA/ESA/Hubble Heritage Team (STScl/
AURA); 32 Shutterstock/John A Davis.
Cards: Front bl Shutterstock/Vadim Sadovski; Back bl Shutterstock/Jaan-Martin Kuusmann;
all other images Kingfisher Artbank.

Front cover: A photorealistic illustration of stars and planets.

CONTENTS

For your free audio download go to
www.panmacmillan.com/audio/
SuperSolarSystem **or** goo.gl/2PnYkl
Happy listening!

Starry night

Look up at the night sky. Can you see the Moon? It is a huge ball of rock that travels around Earth. Can you see any stars? Each star is a giant ball of hot, glowing gas farther away than you can imagine.

Our closest star is the Sun!

FACT ...

Our galaxy could contain up to 500 thousand million stars.

The solar system

The Sun is so large that it pulls planets toward it. Earth and seven other planets travel around the Sun. The Sun and these planets make up our solar system.

Mars

Jupiter

Uranus

SPOTLIGHT: The Sun

Size compared to Earth:	1.3 million times bigger
Distance from Earth:	93 million mi. (150 m km)
Made from:	hot gas
Fact:	4.6 billion years old

Venus

Sun

Mercury

Neptune

Earth

Saturn

You must never look directly at the Sun. Its very strong light can damage your eyes.

Night and day

Earth spins on an imaginary stick called an axis. Imagine a pencil stuck through the middle of a spinning orange.

Day happens when one side of Earth faces the Sun. Night happens when the same side faces away. It takes 24 hours for Earth to spin all the way around once.

Earth takes one year to travel around the Sun. As it moves, different parts of Earth are closer to the Sun. This movement causes the seasons.

FACT ...

As Earth spins round, it is daytime in places that face the Sun. But 12 hours later, the same places face away from the Sun and it is nighttime.

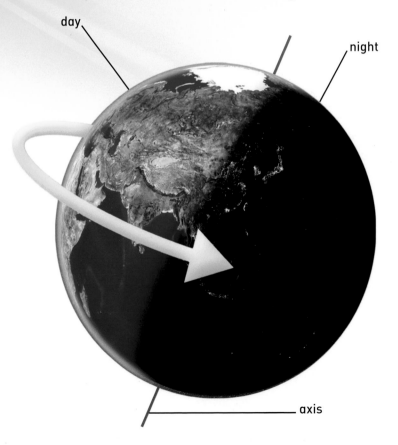

day

night

axis

The Moon

A moon is a ball of rock that travels around a planet. Our Moon is a dry, rocky place with no wind or rain. Nothing can live there.

The Moon orbits Earth.

Look closely at the Moon on a clear night. The dark patches you see are huge flat plains. The light patches are mountains and the rings are craters.

SPOTLIGHT: The Moon

Size compared to Earth: one-seventh of the size

Distance from Earth: 238,855 mi. (384,400km)

Made from: rock

Fact: orbits Earth in 28 days

The changing Moon

The Moon shines at night because light from the Sun bounces off its surface. As the Moon travels around Earth, different parts of the Moon face the Sun and shine.

When the Moon is full, it is facing the Sun.

In the 28 days it takes for the Moon to travel around Earth, the Moon seems to change from a full circle to a thin curve to nothing and back again.

FACT ...

As the Moon travels around Earth it spins slowly, always keeping the same side facing us.

full moon

crescent moon

Moon landings

On July 20, 1969, astronauts Neil Armstrong and Buzz Aldrin became the first people to stand on the Moon.

They traveled across the Moon's surface in a moon buggy and collected rock samples. A total of 12 men have walked on the Moon so far.

A huge rocket blasted the lunar spacecraft into space. It took three days to reach the Moon.

Footprints left on the Moon by the astronauts will last for millions of years because there is no wind or rain to remove them!

Astronauts' bodies are lighter on the Moon so the astronauts bounce when they walk.

Star or planet?

The brightest star in the sky is not a star at all! It looks like a star but it doesn't twinkle. It is Venus, our closest planet and probably the harshest place in the whole solar system.

Moon

You can often see Venus in the sky just after sunset.

SPOTLIGHT: Venus

Size compared to Earth: almost the same size

Distance from Earth: 26 m mi. (42 m km)

Made from: rock

Fact: hottest planet

The surface of Venus is covered with volcanoes and craters.

The Red Planet

Mars is a rocky planet covered with red soil. It is home to Olympus Mons, the largest volcano in the solar system.

Astronauts hope to travel to Mars this century.

SPOTLIGHT: Mars

Size compared to Earth:	about half the size
Distance from Earth:	35 m mi. (56 m km)
Made from:	rocks, soil, and ice
Fact:	called the Red Planet

Robots have been sent to Mars to investigate the planet and to look for signs of life such as fossils.

The Mars rover took photographs of Mars and examined the soil.

Gassy giants

Jupiter and Saturn, the two biggest planets in the solar system, are giant balls of gas and liquid. Jupiter has 67 moons, and storms swirl around its outer layers creating beautiful patterns.

Earth could easily fit inside Jupiter's Great Red Spot.

FACT ...

A hurricane on Jupiter, called the Great Red Spot, has been raging for at least 300 years.

Saturn is the easiest planet to recognize. Lumps of ice and dust spin around this planet, creating rings around its equator.

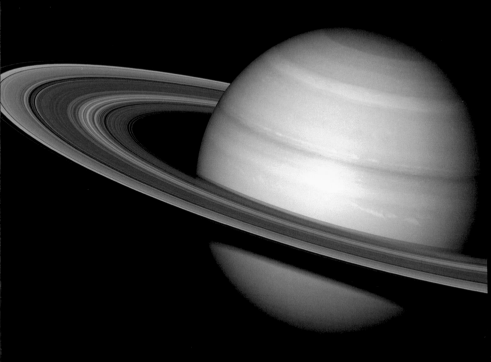

Saturn has 7 rings and 62 moons.

Comets and shooting stars

A comet is a bright lump of ice with a glowing tail. A bright comet is rarely seen in the skies above Earth.

The comet Hale-Bopp was last seen above the Earth on April 1, 1997.

When a lump of space rock enters
Earth's atmosphere it causes a streak
of light in the sky. This is called a
shooting star,
or meteor.

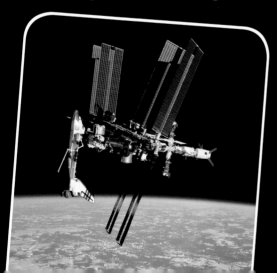

The International
Space Station looks
like a moving star as
it crosses the sky.

Galaxies far, far away

If you look up into the sky on a clear night, you might see a milky-white cloud of stars. This is the Milky Way galaxy—our galaxy. A galaxy is a group of stars. Our Sun is just one of billions of stars in the Milky Way.

You have to be far from bright city lights on a clear night to see the Milky Way.

Scientists think our galaxy—the
Milky Way—looks like this.

our Sun

The universe is made up of countless galaxies stretching out as far as you can imagine.

Each speck of light in this view of deep space is a different galaxy.

Colors and patterns

The Sun looks yellow or orange, but other stars can be different colors. There are red giants, red dwarfs, and blue giants.

Stars are formed inside clouds called nebulas.

Blue giants are a thousand times larger than the Sun, and much hotter.

Red dwarfs are smaller and cooler than our Sun.

People have always loved to make up patterns, called constellations, out of the stars. Imagine drawing lines to join up the stars and form a picture.

Can you find Hercules and Pegasus on this map of the constellations?

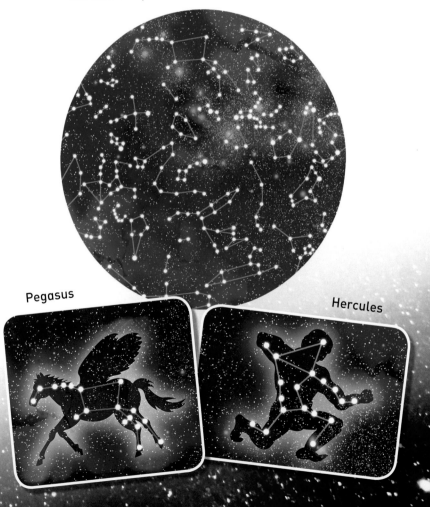

Pegasus

Hercules

Stargazing

If you look at the night sky with the naked eye, you can see stars and planets. If you look with binoculars you can see the moons of Jupiter. If you use a telescope you can see the rings of Saturn.

Scientists use huge telescopes far from city lights to see distant galaxies and comets.

The Hubble Space Telescope orbits Earth and has been taking photographs of deep space for more than 25 years!

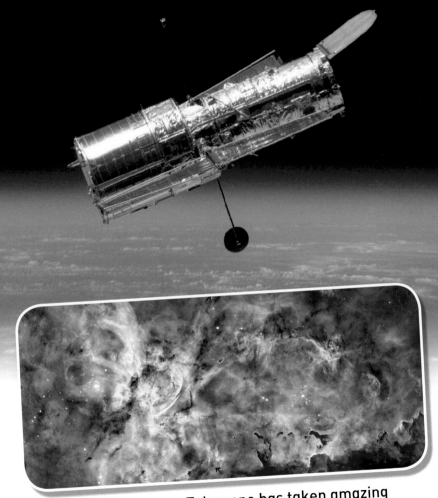

The Hubble Space Telescope has taken amazing pictures of the universe.

GLOSSARY

astronaut A person who travels into space.

atmosphere The layer of gas around a planet.

comet A lump of rock and ice that travels around the Sun.

crater A dent left in a planet or moon by an impact from a giant rock.

equator An imaginary line around the middle of a planet.

fossil The solid rocky remains of an animal or plant that lived long ago.

galaxy A group of millions of stars, planets, gas, and dust that spin together in space.

gas A substance that is not a solid or a liquid.

hurricane A violent spinning windstorm.

lunar To do with the Moon.

Mars rover A robot vehicle that went to Mars and traveled across the planet's surface.

meteor A shooting star caused by a space rock burning up in Earth's atmosphere.

moon A large rocky sphere that travels around a planet.

moon buggy A small vehicle that traveled across the Moon's surface.

nebula A cloud of dust and gas.

orbit To travel around the Sun or a planet.

planet A large, ball-shaped object that travels around a star in space.

season A time of year with certain weather patterns.

telescope An instrument that shows faraway objects more clearly.

INDEX

Collector Card

Collector Card

Collector Card

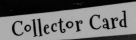

Collector Card

Mars

Robots have landed on Mars but they have found no sign of Martian life.

	SCORE
DIAMETER: 4220 mi. (6790km)	2
MI. (KM) FROM SUN: 142 (227.9) million	4
SURFACE TEMP: -81°F (-63°C)	3
NUMBER OF MOONS: 2	2

Jupiter

A ball of gas and liquid with swirling storms and many moons.

	SCORE
DIAMETER: 86,000 mi. (140,000km)	8
MI. (KM) FROM SUN: 484 (778.4) million	5
SURFACE TEMP: -166°F (-110°C)	2
NUMBER OF MOONS: 67	10

Saturn

Many moons and rings of dust and ice spin around Saturn's equator.

	SCORE
DIAMETER: 73,000 mi. (120,000km)	7
MI. (KM) FROM SUN: 890 million (1.4 billion)	6
SURFACE TEMP: -220°F (-140°C)	2
NUMBER OF MOONS: 62	9

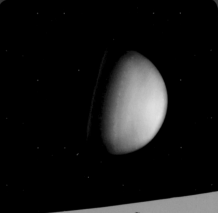

Uranus

This blue-green planet has faint rings and is tilted on its side.

	SCORE
DIAMETER: 32,000 mi. (51,000km)	6
MI. (KM) FROM SUN: 1.8 (2.9) billion	7
SURFACE TEMP: -322°F (-197°C)	1
NUMBER OF MOONS: 27	6